THIS JOURNAL BELONGS TO:

____

PAPERLUSH

PRESS

PAPERLUSH

PRESS

Made in the USA
Middletown, DE
23 March 2021

36103736R00068